Make Your Own Candle the Easy Way

Your Complete Guide to the Art of Candle Making, Including Dyes, Oils, Waxes and How to Sell It for Profit

Kelly Kohn

PUBLISHED BY:
Kelly Kohn
Copyright © 2012

All rights reserved.

No part of this publication may be copied, reproduced in any format, by any means, electronic or otherwise, without prior consent from the copyright owner and publisher of this book.

Disclaimer
The information contained in this book is for general information purposes only. The information is provided by the authors and while we endeavor to keep the information up to date and correct, we make no representations or warranties of any kind, express or implied, about the completeness, accuracy, reliability, suitability or availability with respect to the book or the information, products, services, or related graphics contained in the book for any purpose. Any reliance you place on such information is therefore strictly at your own risk.

The Joy of Candle Making

Fire has long been admired by humans. It has been part of ceremonies, social gatherings, and meditation for over two millennia (if not longer). Making your own fire (candles) can change prayer into devotion and relaxation into meditation. Candles can turn a bubble bath into a sensual, relaxing experience. You can decorate your house with candles or hand them out as special gifts. The fact that you have made the candle gives them special importance. You can create candles that are just meant to look pretty or turn them into a beautiful, scented experience by adding essential oils. You can purchase candles for all of these reasons, but if you make them yourself, you can save money and ensure that they are made with natural ingredients.

Making candles at home is not only fun, but it is also a great way to experiment with different wax types, mold types, colors, and essential oil mixtures. Making candles is a creative process that can give you great satisfaction and a deep connection to the product you have made. If it is your first time making candles, start simple. As you become more proficient, you can experiment with different waxes, wicks, molds, scents, and styles. Once you've experimented and created your own recipes, you'll find that the possibilities for your candles and their ingredients are endless.

Besides using them to decorate your home or as gifts for friends and family, you can sell your candles. Some shops will take your candles on commission, and you can also sell them online. Candle making is a hobby that can lead to personal and monetary satisfaction. It just takes time and love to grow it from a hobby into a business.

Table of Contents

Make Your Own Candle the Easy Way 1

The Joy of Candle Making 2

Table of Contents 2

Chapter 1: Candle Making Basics *6*

    Creating a Mold 8

    Candle Dyes 8

    Essential Oils 9

    Using Candles to Make Candles 10

    Making Your Candle 10

    Chunk Candles 14

    Create Your Chunks 14

    Over Dipped Candles 15

    Hand Dipped Candles 17

    Cleaning Your Instruments 18

    Reusing Old Candles 19

Chapter 2: Candle Making Ideas *19*

    Teacup Candles 20

    Silver Plated Container Candles 20

    Candles in Tins 20

    Whipped Wax 21

    Free Candle Molds 21

Chapter 3: Using Essential Oils *22*

    Scent Categories 22

    Scent Notes 23

    Blending Your Oils 24

    Tips for Essential Oils 25

    Substituting Scents 25

    Scent Qualities 26

    Vanilla 26

    Lavender 26

Orange 27

Ginger 28

Peppermint 28

Cinnamon 29

Essential Oil Recipes 30

Light Lemon 30

Pleasing Jasmine 30

Grapefruit Sunrise 30

Basil 30

Chapter 4:   Wicks and Waxes *31*

Wicks 31

Cored Wicks 32

Braided Wicks 32

Candle Wick Tabs 33

Different Waxes 33

Natural Waxes 33

Artificial Waxes 34

Wax Additives 35

Wax Temperatures 36

Chapter 5:   Using Your Own Beeswax *37*

Chapter 6:   Types of Candles *38*

Pillar Candles 39

Floating Candles 39

Votive Candles 39

Taper Candles 39

Container or Filled Candles 40

Tea light Candles 40

Gel Candles 40
Birthday Candles 40

Chapter 7: Selling Your Candles 41
In Person 42
Choosing a Venue 42
Creating Your Booth 44
On Consignment 47
Online 48

Chapter 8: Candle Making Books and Videos 48
Books 49
Videos 49
Websites 50

Chapter 9: More Tips 51
Burn Rate 53
Some Tips When Working with Gel Wax 54
Embedding Items in Gel Wax 55
Using Essential Oils and Colors with Gel Wax 55
How to Choose a Glass Container 55
Tips for Cleaning Up 56
Safety 56

Chapter 10: Troubleshooting 57
Problem: Wick Burns Straight, Leaving a Cavity in the Center 57
Problem: Candle Changes Color 57
Problem: Candle Won't Burn 57
Problem: Candle's Surface is Cracked 58
Problem: Candle Drips 58
Problem: Candle Stops Burning 58

Problem: Candle Won't Release from Mold 59

Problem: Excess Wax is Left on the Container Walls 60

Problem: Outside of the Candle Looks Dusty 60

Problem: There are Pits and Bubbles in the Wax 60

Problem: Colored Layers Bleed 61

Problem: Mold is Leaking 62

Problem: There are Dark Spots on Top of the Candle 62

Problem: The Candle is Mottled 62

Problem: The Flame Sputters 62

Problem: Sides of Candle Cave in 63

Problem: The Candle is Smoking 63

Problem: The Flame is Weak or the Wick is Drowning in Wax 63

Problem: Wax is too Brittle 63

Problem: There are Visible Lines on the Outside of the Candle 64

Problem: The Scent of the Candle is not Strong Enough 64

Glossary 66

Chapter 1: Candle Making Basics

Before you start your candle-making adventure, you'll need to be sure you have the right items. You'll need to find pots that won't be used for cooking food. You can use some old pots you have on hand that you will need to retire from cooking or buy some from garage sales or thrift stores, or from cooking shops or craft stores.

Store them away from regular cooking utensils, so they don't get mixed up.

Things you can find around the house:

- Candy, Candle or Meat Thermometer *(Just make sure it reaches 220 degrees Fahrenheit)*

- Double Boiler *(You can use any old pot and any glass or metal dish for the top. You can also use an old coffee can as the pot you put the wax in)*

- Kitchen Scale

- Pouring Device *(A glass measuring cup would work well)*

- Wax Paper

- Wooden Spoon *(Used for stirring melting wax. Make sure it is only used for wax)*

Things you can buy at a craft store:

- Candle Molds

- Candle Wax

- Candle Wicks

- Candle Wick Tabs

- Candle Dye

- Mold release

- Mold Sealer

- Wax additives

- Essential Oils (See USING ESSENTIAL OILS)

Creating a Mold

You don't have to buy any molds to make a candle, you can make your own easily with items you have around your house. You can make molds out of cardboard, paper milk cartons (not the plastic gallon or half-gallon jugs), and soda pop cans. To use the cans or cartons, make a hole in the bottom center and cut the top off of the container. You can use unused chopsticks as the skewer for the top. Make your candle with these containers the same way you would for any candle.

Making a candle mold out of corrugated cardboard is super easy, too! Just coat one side of the cardboard with cooking oil and shape it into your desired shape. The great thing about making cardboard molds is that your own creativity is your only real boundary. After you've shaped it, with oiled side in, tape it up with shaping tape. Use as much tape as you need to seal any openings and to keep it together under the stress of the cooling wax. Next, make a lid for your creation and make a hole in the center for the wick. You can make the lid out of cardboard or use an old, plastic or metal lid. Use mold sealer to secure the bottom of the mold to the lid. Now, use this mold the same way you'd use a purchased mold in making your candle.

Candle Dyes

Wax doesn't usually come in assorted colors; candle makers have to add their own colors. They come in liquid, powdered, and solid forms. Adding dye is done slowly, a little at a time until you are able to reach your desired color. Most dyes have instructions on how to use them printed or inserted into/on the packaging.

Liquid dye is a lot like food coloring, but don't use food coloring to color your candle. Since it is a liquid, it blends easily, but it is also concentrated, so only a bit of dye will be needed. For instance, some liquid dyes require only ½ an ounce to color 100 pounds of wax!

Solid dye usually consists of chunks of wax and color pigment. They are normally referred to as color chips or blocks. They are cut up and added to melted wax, and then stirred to fully integrate the color into the melted wax. You can add as much or as little as you need. Some chips will dye a pound of wax a medium to light shade of your desired color.

Powdered dyes usually need to be dissolved in stearic acid, which is a fatty acid that needs to be melted before you add the powder. Powdered dyes are the most concentrated form of candle coloring and only a small amount needs to be added to your melted wax.

Essential Oils

Essential oils are pure essences or aromatic plants. They are not synthetic, which means they are not artificially produced and won't contain any suspicious ingredients. Essentials oils are the heart of the plant and can enhance your spiritual, physical, and emotional well-being. However, adding essential oils to your candle isn't just about adding fragrance—it's about experiencing the fragrance and connecting with it. It's about finding the exact right amount for the project. It's important that you buy your essential oils from a reputable dealer to insure that you are getting 100% pure oils and no synthetics. Synthetics can contain surprise ingredients, some of which can cause allergic reactions or contain carcinogens. They could also be toxic to your skin. Also, a candle made with essential oils is a pure aromatic experience and will create a candle that is unique to you and your style.

When buying your essential oils, be sure you read the labels carefully. It should state the botanical name, how it was extracted, where it was from, and how the plant was cultivated. They also vary in scent depending on the origin of the plant, how good the distiller is, and how it was stored. If you are looking for the pure extract, stay away from oils that are diluted in oil. One way to find out if it is diluted with oil is by placing a drop of the oil on a piece of paper and letting it evaporate. If it leaves an oily mark behind, then it has been diluted with oil.

Using Candles to Make Candles

You can save the ends of used candles for use in your own candles. Keep like colors together and when you have enough, melt them and pour them into your mold. You will need to use a slotted spoon to take out the wicks or candle wick tabs that remain.

Making Your Candle

Before you begin making candles, get a notebook or create a file for your notes. You should keep notes on wax combinations, essential oil combinations, and wick and candle combinations. Keep track of which combinations work best for you, how long you need to melt certain waxes, and how much oil or color you put into your candles based on their size and shape to create the perfect combination for you. This will come in handy when you really get into the candle making hobby, as you may forget just how you created that lilac-scented votive that smelled and looked so marvelous. If you keep notes during your process and remark upon the outcomes in those notes, you will find it simple to recreate your successes and not your failures.

Before you begin the process of candle making, be sure you have all of your instruments at hand.

1. Spread wax paper over your work surface, just in case you spill or drip the wax during pouring.

2. Determine how much wax you'll need for your project.

An easy way to figure out how much wax you need involves mathematics. You can convert water to wax (not magically, *mathematically*) by measuring. Using your kitchen scale, weigh the mold before adding the water so you can subtract the weight of the mold and set your scale accordingly. Fill your mold with water and weigh it on the kitchen scale. This number will tell you how much wax you'll need for that one container. Therefore, if your mold holds 14 ounces of water, you'd need to melt approximately 14 ounces of wax to fill the mold. It also depends on the type of wax you are using. There may be some paperwork with your wax that tells you how many ounces a pound will equal when melted, but there may not be. This number differs by wax type.

For instance, 1 pound of paraffin will equal about 20 oz. of liquid wax, while 1 pound of beeswax will equal about 16oz of liquid wax.

3. Put your wax into a garbage bag and begin breaking it up with a hammer. If necessary, use a screwdriver. Break the wax into small chunks.

4. Put the wax into the top pot of a double boiler.

    You can make your own double boiler with a glass bowl and a metal pot, or purchase a double boiler, either new from a store or used from a thrift store or garage sale. If you have an old one lying around that you aren't using for cooking, you can use that one too. You can also use an old coffee can to melt the wax in the water bath; just don't add it to the water until it has started to boil. Once the water is boiling, add the coffee can of wax chips. Stir occasionally to prevent clumping and to help chunks of wax melt. Whatever you do, **don't melt the wax directly over heat**. Like melting chocolate, it can scorch the wax. Unlike chocolate, wax will flame up when scorched, which can be dangerous to you, your kitchen, and your utensils.

5. Place the pan on the stove and boil the water. Once the wax begins melting, place your candy/candle thermometer in the wax. **Do not let the bottom of the thermometer touch the bottom of the dish**, though. I did this once, on accident, while

making candy, and the thermometer exploded. It was terrifying, and it ruined the candy.

6. Turn the heat down to medium-low once the water is boiling and let the water continue at a gentle boil. Check it now and then to be sure that your water doesn't boil away. Add water as necessary.

7. Prepare your mold and your wick.

    Lightly coat the inside of your mold with the product called mold release (available at most craft stores) and set aside. Next, cut your wick to the desired length for your mold. It should be a bit longer than your mold. (See WICKS for information on wick lengths and types.) There should be a hole at the bottom of your mold; thread the wick through. Cover the hole and secure the wick with a product called mold sealer and pull the wick straight up through the mold. Put a metal or wooden skewer, which will come with purchased molds, or a straight length of a hard material that is larger than the diameter of your mold over the top of the mold. Making sure the wick is taut and straight; wrap it around the skewer, so it will remain that way.

    If you are making a container candle, use a wick that has a wick tab attached to the bottom. Pour a little of your melted wax into the candle—enough to cover the tab and entire bottom. Center the wick and attach it to the skewer. Allow the wax to set just enough to keep the wick in place before pouring the rest of your wax into the container.

8. Add your wax additives when your wax is at the right temperature, (see WAX TEMPERATURES to find out the right temperature for your container or mold type). You can start adding any additives or colors to your wax. If you are going to add any essential oils, wait until you are ready to pour the wax, so you don't lose any of your scent to heat.

9. Pour your melted wax into your mold but only fill it 90%; do not fill it to the top.

    You can either pour the wax directly in your mold or use a ladle or your preferred pouring device. Alternatively, you can pour it into a glass measuring cup since the metal ladle may get too hot after a while and pouring straight from the pan or bowl can be messy.

10. Pour unused wax into a clean, tin can and set it aside.

11. Tap the sides of the mold to release any air bubbles.

    As the wax dries/hardens, you may notice an indentation in the center of the candle, towards the wick. Don't worry, this is normal and will be remedied with that wax you have in the tin can.

12. Put the tin can into the boiling water and melt the wax again. This is your re-pour wax.

13. Fill the indentation with the excess wax. Don't overfill, however, since the drying wax will form a line around the outside of the candle and mar the way it looks.

14. Let the wax cool inside the mold.

15. Remove the skewer and the mold sealer once your candle is cool to the touch.

16. Let the candle cool for 24 hours and take it out of the mold. The candle should easily slide out of the mold once it is cooled. Tip it over and slide it out.

    If, for some reason, it doesn't want to budge, you can place the mold into your freezer for about 5 to 10 minutes. Remove it from the freezer and turn it over. Now, the candle should slide right out.

If you are making a container candle, skip step 15.

17. Leave your candle to rest for a day before lighting.

Chunk Candles

Making chunk candles is done by cutting wax from already scented and dyed candles and placing them in a mold. After you place the chunks in your mold, you pour un-dyed wax over the chunks. Using paraffin here is a good idea, since it is a less opaque wax than most and will allow the candle chunks to show through.

Create Your Chunks

You can do this process as much as you like, so that you have multiple colors and scents to work with.

1. Melt your wax to about 198 degrees Fahrenheit and add your color and scent(s). (See MAKING YOUR CANDLE for details on how this process works).

2. Pour your wax into a shallow container, like a cookie sheet with sides, either metal or plastic. Pour it back and forth to distribute the heat evenly.

3. Allow the wax to cool until it is set, but make sure it is still flexible.

4. Cut the wax into your desired chunk shape. You can cut it into squares using a knife in a crisscross pattern or use a cookie cutter for different shapes, like hearts or gingerbread men.

5. Let the wax cool completely; the more brittle, the better it will work. You can chill the wax in the refrigerator to make it even more brittle.

6. Overturn sheet onto a piece of waxed paper—it should come off easily and break apart at the points you cut easily. If they are stuck together, you can snap them apart with your hands.

7. Put the wick in your mold as you normally would and then stack the chunks in your desired pattern.

8. Heat the wax you are going to pour over the chunks. This is called overpour wax. Choose a wax that is translucent. You can alternate the heat of the overpour wax to create different textures. Hotter wax will allow the chunks' color to bleed into the overpour wax; cooler wax can introduce bubbles and different textures to your candle. You can fill the wax until it covers your chunks completely, or you can leave a few chunks poking through the top of the candle.

Finish it as you would a normal candle. You should not need to re-pour the wax in a chunk candle as you do in a normal candle, as that sinkhole around the wick does not generally form in a chunk candle.

Over Dipped Candles

You need to use a container that is long and cylindrical to create over dipped candles. You can purchase a special container from craft stores, or use a large coffee can that is deep enough for your candle. This technique is used to add a new layer of color to an already made candle. Keep the temperature of the new wax around 150 to 160 degrees Fahrenheit. This temperature may differ depending on the type of wax of which the original candle was made. If the wax is too hot, it may melt the original candle or it may add layers that are far too thin. If it is too cool, it will come out lumpy.

1. Choose the candle you want to overdip and the colors you want to add to the candle. These can be the same color as the original (useful if you are trying to salvage the candle) or

different colored waxes so that you can have layers of color in your candle.

2. Heat desired wax and color to 150 to 160 degrees Fahrenheit. Color for overdipped candles is usually more intense than for regular candles, so you will need to add more of your color additive than you normally would.

3. Pour your melted wax into your dipping container. Keep the container in hot water and stir often to maintain temperature. Alternatively, you can place the container in a pot of hot, boiling water.

4. Hold the original candle by the wick and, for the first dip, hold it in the new wax for at least 30 seconds.

5. Allow the candle to cool between dips. This can be done by placing the candle into cold water immediately. Before going back for another dip, wipe away excess water.

6. Dip the candle back into the wax and then into the water as often as necessary to attain the desired thickness of the color. The subsequent dips in both the wax and the water should be quickly done so that the candle does not cool too much. Wax sticks best to wax that is warm.

Dip your candles in a smooth motion to avoid lumping. Don't overfill your container with new wax to avoid spills. This technique is great for candle projects that have seams that need to be removed, to cover any embellishments (using a translucent wax) that you've added, creating candles that "glow" (adding color over a translucent candle can create this effect), and to create a carved candle that shows multiple colors through the cuts.

Hand Dipped Candles

The oldest method of making candles is to hand dip them. This method works best using a paraffin wax. Follow the directions for melting wax and adding colors and dyes in MAKING YOUR CANDLES.

1. Make sure the temperature of the wax stays at about 160 degrees Fahrenheit.

2. Cut your wick to your desired length times two (you will make two candles), plus a little extra length so you can hold it. For instance, if you want two six inch candles measure out 12 inches of wick and add at least three inches to it. Double the wick around the finger you are going to hold it with, whichever one is comfortable for you.

3. Dip the wick into the wax for a few seconds and then lift it out. At first, it may be a bit hard as the wick is lighter than the wax and doesn't want to sink down into the wax, but don't worry: once the wicks start accumulating wax, they'll stop floating on top.

4. Allow the wax to cool between dips and make sure they never touch. Continue dipping and cooling. After the first few layers, you can dip the candles into a cooling bath after each dip, but it isn't necessary.

5. Repeat the dipping and cooling process until the candles are as thick as you want them to be. If they have lumps, you can roll the candles on a smooth surface, while they are still warm, to even out the lumps.

6. Heat the wax until it is 182 degrees Fahrenheit and dip the candles one more time for a couple of seconds and remove. Allow them to cool.

7. Use a sharp knife to trim excess wax and to make a straight bottom. You can do this while they are warm to the touch, but not yet completely cool. If you wait until they are completely cool, they may fracture.

8. Hang the candles to dry. A drying rack for clothes can be used (as long as it's never used for clothes again).

9. Cut the wick. Wait 24 hours before lighting.

Cleaning Your Instruments

Keep your molds, pots, spoons, and containers clean before each use to prevent problems with new candles. This method works best with metal and glassware that can be used for baking. All you need are paper towels and an old, unused cookie sheet.

1. Get all of the tools you will be cleaning.

2. Get out your cookie sheet and towels.

3. Make three to four layers of paper towels over your cookie sheet.

4. Put all of the tools onto the paper towels. Make sure molds and containers are upside down.

5. Put your oven at its lowest setting, even the "keep warm" setting will work.

6. Put your cookie sheet filled with tools into the oven for five minutes. Check to see if the tools are clear of wax. If all of the wax hasn't melted, put it in for a few more minutes and check again.

7. Remove the sheet from the oven, carefully.

8. Wipe away any leftover wax with a paper towel while the wax is still warm.

If you are using molds and tools that can't be put in direct heat, put them in the freezer for about 20 minutes. The wax will start to crack and chip away. You can also soak them in a pot of very hot water for a few minutes, and wipe away the warm wax.

Reusing Old Candles

You can melt down old candles the same way you melt down your wax for creating candles. Use a double boiler method to melt the wax. If you can, remove the wick and wick tabs, and any dirty parts of the candle before melting. If you can't remove the wick and wick tabs first, don't worry, you can fish them out as it melts. If you are melting down an old container candle, just place the container (as long as it is glass or metal) into the pot of boiling water. Make your candles the way you normally would.

Make sure you keep candles that have similar scents and similar colors together. When melting down colored candles, make sure you mix it well before pouring so that the colors blend well.

Chapter 2: Candle Making Ideas

You can use just about anything to make your candles. Reusing items will not only save you money, but it will also help you create unique candles to give away or to sell. Most of the items in these ideas can be found in thrift stores, at garage sales, or in your own home.

Teacup Candles

You can find all sorts of teacups at thrift stores; many are priced nice and cheap. Find the styles you like—they don't have to match—and stock up on teacups until you feel like you have enough. If you don't want to purchase new wax, buy a lot of used candles from thrift stores and melt them.

Items needed: Normal candle making equipment including wicks, assorted teacups, and if you have them—old candles.
Melt wax. Prime the wick and place it into the teacup. Use your skewer to stabilize the wick. When wax is melted, pour it into the teacups. Stop at least a half inch below the rim and allow to cool. Set unused wax aside. When teacup candles are cooled, melt the unused wax and level off the candle. Once they are cool, remove skewers and trim wicks. This doesn't stop with teacups. You can make mug candles as well!

Silver Plated Container Candles

You can also find assorted silver plated dishware at thrift stores. It may be tarnished, but you can buff it to a brilliant shine after you get it home. If they come with lids, that's a plus. Just make your wax as you normally would, prime your wick, and secure it. Remember to make sure you measure the container and know what type of wick to use so they burn properly. Make the candle as you normally would and let cool. These make perfect, fancy-style gifts.

Candles in Tins

You may also be able to find tins at thrift stores, though they get snatched up pretty quickly sometimes. Find out when your thrift store puts out new items and be sure to get there first. You can use old medicine tins, tea tins, and sardine cans— whatever tin you can find. Since these are container candles, you don't need to worry about setting the mold release or sealing the wick hole, just place your wick, melt the wax, and pour.

Whipped Wax

Making whipped wax is easier than you may have thought. You can use it to make birthday cake candles, root beer float candles, ice cream sundae candles, cupcakes candles—really, anything you can think up. Melt your wax like you normally would. Since this is probably going to be on top of your candle, make sure you make that base wax first. Allow the wax you want to whip to cool until it forms a skin on top. Get out an old egg beater, and whip it until it becomes frothy. If you want a whiter look, you can add white corn flour, but be careful, as it tends to clump up. When it is frothy, spoon it onto your candle and allow the wax to cool.

Free Candle Molds

Free is always nice, however, this is kind of a misnomer. These things may not really be free, because at some point, you paid money for the item. You can find candle molds in your trash can. Old tin cans, juice boxes, baby food jars (container candle), and paper milk cartons make great molds for your candles.

Other container ideas include

- Small aquariums (very small)
- Pop cans with the tops taken off
- Jell-O molds
- Aluminum foil that you've made into a shape
- Old buckets
- Old teapots
- Terracotta flower pots

- Hurricane vases

- Old light covers

You can also use household items to give your candles a unique look. You can use corrugated cardboard inside your mold to add the corrugated look to your candle. Make sure you are placing it in the mold corrugated side facing in. You can line the inside of your mold with Popsicle sticks strategically placed. Just be sure that you add the mold release to the cardboard or Popsicle sticks so they do not become part of the candle.

Nearly any hollow container that can withstand the heat of melted wax can be used as a mold. If you decide to use Mason jars, make container candles, especially if the jar has a lip, which can make sliding the candle out difficult.

You can even use old egg shells to make small candles. After Easter, when eating the colored eggs, try to keep half of the shell intact. Place your primed wick into the egg shell and pour your wax into the shell. Use a low temperature wax so you don't have to pour wax in that could be too hot for the shell.

Chapter 3: Using Essential Oils

This section will give you an overview of the things you need to know about essential oils to make it easier to use them. We will talk about scent categories, scent notes, how to blend your oils, tips, scent substitutions, and what qualities some scents will bring to your candle.

Scent Categories

Scents come in categories. They are camphorous, citrus, floral, herbal, resinous, spicy, and woodsy, and minty. Scents normally fall into at least one of these categories.

- Camphorous scents are pungent and sharp. This includes pine, tea tree, and eucalyptus.

- Citrus scents are fresh and clean smelling. These include grapefruit, lemon, orange, and lime.

- Floral scents are soft and flowery. Included in this category are jasmine, lavender, and rose.

- Herbal scents smell like herbs and are very intense. This includes the scent of basil, rosemary, and sage.

- Resinous scents are biblical, usually made with gums or resins. This includes the scents frankincense and myrrh.

- Spicy scents are sharp. Included in the category are the scents of pepper, cinnamon, and nutmeg.

- Woodsy scents give off a smell of freshly cut wood. Like being in a forest, you will smell cedar and sandalwood.

- Minty scents are cool and fresh. They include peppermint and spearmint.

Scent Notes

If you think about scent as you would think about music, you get this analogy. The top notes are the head notes of the scent. They smell light and fresh, and are usually the first thing you'll notice about the smell; however, it is a scent that dissipates quickly. The middle notes are the heart of the scent; they are rooted deeper into the scent and form the body of the scent, as in music. The base notes last longer and are a bit heavier than the top and middle. They dominate the scent after the first two have dissipated. They are usually rich and help ground the blend, bringing it all together into one satisfying, sensual song.

Thinking about the notes of your scent with the analogy of music can help you create blends that are deep and moving. Use the scent categories to create your blend in relation to where they lie in your candle's song. It's important to remember that the blend will alter as it ages and may change the initial scent you were looking for. Age the blend for a day or two and smell it again before using it. The result may surprise you.

Blending Your Oils

You don't need to be an expert at scents to create your own blend, though at first it may be easier to use recipes. Even though recipes may prove useful, all you need to know is what you like, and what works for you. Acquaint yourself with your scents. Wander around in a shop that sells essential oils and explore the scents you like. Make notes on which scents strike you as calming, grounding, or sensual. Familiarize yourself with the different dimensions and qualities that the oils have. Experience the oils and learn from that experience.

When you've finally found your notes, blend them in a glass bottle. You will need different droppers for your oils, so that the oils do not become mixed in their individual containers. Don't switch the caps on the bottles. Color coding them may help you keep track of what cap belongs to which scent.

The following steps will help you blend your chosen scents:

1. Select the oils you want to use. While there are no rules about how many scents to blend together, beginners should stick to three to four in their first blending forays.

2. Drop an equal amount of oil drops into your glass bottle. For instance, if scent one got two drops, scents two and three do as well.

3. Shake your bottle. Open the cap and smell the results to test the fragrance.

4. Introduce additional drops into the mixture a few at a time to achieve your desired effect. After each few drops, shake, and test.

Always keep notes on your blends. Include which oils you used, and how many drops you put into the blend. Write down your reasons for choosing your oils. Make a reflection of your perception of the blend, both when you first blend it and after it has aged.

Tips for Essential Oils

- Store your essential oils in a dark glass bottle in a cool, dark storage area.

- Label your oils and your blends clearly. Be specific. Add the labels and information for the blends and oils in your notebook.

- Don't store the oil with the rubber stopper tops covering the bottles. The rubber can turn to a gummy consistency and ruin the oil.

- Pay attention to the safety information provided by the essential oil, as some oils can harm you if it gets on your skin, is swallowed, or used during pregnancy.

Substituting Scents

You can substitute some scents for others, depending on what is available.

Substitute:
- Peru Balsam for vanilla oil

- Lavender for chamomile

- Clove for cinnamon
- Grapefruit for lemon
- Spearmint for peppermint
- Sweet orange for tangerine

Scent Qualities

Vanilla

- Mixes well with clove, sandalwood, and cinnamon. The sweet smell of vanilla can calm nerves, reduce muscle tension, and revitalize your body.
- Can make the blend earthier when blended with clove and spicier when blended with rose, but vanilla oil is pricy.

Lavender

- Blends well with chamomile, citrus, lemongrass, and rose. It is a disinfectant that enhances sleep, loosens congestions, reduces muscle tension and pain, repels insects and soothes and heals skin.
- Can make the following scents more herbal
    - Black pepper
    - Chamomile
    - Cinnamon

- Eucalyptus
- Ginger
- Grapefruit
- Lemongrass
- Lime
- Nutmeg
- Orange
- Peppermint
- Rose
- Sandalwood

Orange

- Mixes well with cinnamon, juniper, and sandalwood. It is an antidepressant that purifies the body and mind, reduces muscle tension, and can relive anxiety and fear.
- Can heighten the scent of grapefruit and mandarin orange.
- Can freshen the scent of
    - Cardamom
    - Clove
    - Lime
    - Nutmeg

- Rose
- Sandalwood

Ginger

- Blends well with lavender, lemon, lime, orange, and sandalwood. It can enhance appetite, heightens the senses, relieves stress, and soothes the body and mind.
- Can make these scents spicier
    - Black pepper
    - Cardamom
    - Clove
    - Frankincense
    - Orange
    - Peppermint
    - Rose
    - Can heighten the scent of lemon

Peppermint

- Mixes well with clove, eucalyptus, lime and marjoram. The scent can reduce fatigue, repel insects, and stimulate the nerves. Other uses of peppermint include its ability to reduce inflammation, loosen congestion, and improve digestion.
- Can make the scent of lavender more herbal.

- Heightens the scents of
    - Basil
    - Lemon
    - Rosemary

Cinnamon

- Blends well with coriander, jasmine, lemon, and sandalwood. It is considered an aphrodisiac, can enhance mental clarity, and stimulate circulation. Other uses of cinnamon include its ability to improve digestion.
- Heightens the scent of clove and nutmeg.
- Can make these scents spicier
    - Black pepper
    - Cardamom
    - Frankincense
    - Orange
    - Rosemary
    - Vanilla

Essential Oil Recipes

Here are a few recipes to get your started on your blending adventure.

Light Lemon

This recipe works well with 3 inch diameter round pillars.
1 drop lavender
3 drops lemon
1 drop lemongrass

Pleasing Jasmine

You can use this scent in any pillar candle.
2 drops jasmine
1 drop rose
1 drop Ylang-ylang

Grapefruit Sunrise

The refreshing scent of grapefruit will relieve stress and fatigue.
2 drops grapefruit
1 drop orange
1 drop vanilla

Basil

Basil has a pleasant aroma that can revitalize your body and purify your mind.
3 drops basil
2 drops lavender
1 drop rosemary

Chapter 4:   Wicks and Waxes

Wicks

Making candles is not as simple as melting wax and pouring it into a container. Depending on the type of candle you want to make, you will have to choose the wick type, as well as which wax to use. The wicks available on the market all have different properties which will help aid the wax to burn more efficiently. You can buy wicks that are primed or unprimed.

To prime your wicks, soak the wick in melted wax for five minutes. Take the wick out of the wax and let it cool by laying it straight on a piece of waxed paper.

The size and diameter of the wick you need to use is determined by the size of your candle and the type of wax that you are using. For instance a long burning wax like beeswax would require a larger-sized wick diameter. Think of the wicks in this way: small-sized wick = thin, medium-sized wick = average, large-sized wick = thick. You would use a thin wick for a candle that is two inches or below in diameter. You would use an average wick for candles that are two to three inches in diameter. You would use a thick wick for candles that are three to four inches in diameter.

The length of your wick depends on the height of your candle. You determine the length by measuring the height of the mold and adding two inches. If you want to create an embellished wick, you'd add more than two inches to the height of the mold.

There are many different types of wicks available at craft stores. Wicks are usually either braided or cored. There are numerous varieties of these wick types available. All of the varieties burn differently and are used for different candle types and sizes. It is up to you to find the wick types that work best for your creations. Remember to keep notes on how each wick works for you.

Cored Wicks

Cored wicks are wicks that tend to be braided with a core of cotton, paper or zinc to help keep the wicks upright. These types of wicks are best used for container candles, votive candles, pillar candles and novelty candles that require a wick to stay upright.

Paper-Core Wicks are usually used for votives, tea lights, and container candles. They smoke more than other wicks, however.

Wire-Core Wicks can also be used for container, votive, and tea light candles. Some can be purchased with tabs already attached. Most are made from zinc, but be aware that some may be made with lead, which can be a health hazard.

Cotton-Core Wicks are also best in the above candle types. They create a slightly curled flame that creates an even burning circumference. It doesn't smoke as badly as the paper-core variety.

Braided Wicks

Flat-Braid Wicks work best for dipped candles. This wick is slightly pliable, which allows for an even burn and prevents the mushrooming effect that is often found in some cheaper store bought candles.

Square Braid Wicks work best in pillar candles and are not as pliable as the flat-braid wick. Unlike the flat-braid, however, this wick also works very well in a tapered candle or any candle that is made of beeswax.

Candle Wick Tabs

Candle wick tabs can be used as a way to anchor the wick to the bottom of your candle. They are small metal disks that can be attached to the bottom of the wick. Instead of threading the wick through a hole in the bottom center of your mold, cover that hole and pour a small amount of your melted wax into the mold. Center the disk in the wax and it will be secured as the wax cools. Wrap the top of the wick around your stick, and pour the remaining wax into the mold.

Different Waxes

There are different waxes for different reasons. Aromatic candles made with a softer wax seem more fragrant because soft wax doesn't seal as tightly as hard wax, allowing the scents to permeate the air around it. However, soft wax works best in container candles, as free-standing candles would quickly lose their shape.

Natural Waxes

If you are looking to use all-natural ingredients for your candles, there are natural alternatives. You can use beeswax, vegetable-based waxes, or bayberry wax. You can mix wax types to create the wax consistency you desire.

Beeswax works well in containers and for dipped candles. It has a beautiful burn and even has its very own aroma. It's stickier than other waxes and usually requires a larger-sized wick. The stickiness could be a problem if you are trying to take it out of a mold. It has a low melting point, and when burned, tends to melt directly down the middle. It works best when mixed with higher temperature waxes. It is also the most expensive wax.

Vegetable-based waxes are made from different bases. They can be made from soybeans, jojoba beans, palm wax, and other vegetables. This wax is normally used in container candles. Candles made with a vegetable-based wax burn long and clean. You may have a hard time finding these waxes at a craft store, but they can be found online.

Bayberry wax is created by boiling the berries from the bush. The wax is a sage-green color and has a natural, spicy aroma. A lot of the bayberry candles available at the market are mislabeled—they are usually made from normal wax and then have the bayberry fragrance added. If you choose to order or buy bayberry wax, check to make sure it is authentic.

Artificial Waxes

Artificial waxes may have a natural ingredient or two, but the majority of the ingredients are man-made. Two artificial waxes that are commonly used by candle makers are paraffin wax and gel wax.

Paraffin wax is made from mineral oil. It is cheap and easy to find. It works well for molded candles and has a low oil content which means it has a higher melting point. It is translucent and works best for over dipping candles and coating chunk candles. It smokes, however, and doesn't burn as cleanly as the natural waxes listed. Some people feel nauseous after making candles with paraffin, and it is believed that the reason for this is the fact that the wax is made from petroleum and the carbon from the burnt carbon ends up in the air. It may leave black soot on surfaces.

Gel wax is also made from mineral oil, but it has been thickened with a polymer, creating a smooth wax that has a longer burn rate than paraffin or natural waxes. It is generally clear in color, but color can be added to it. It doesn't melt, as wax does, as it is already a liquid, but heating it does cause it to become a thinner consistency. It has a higher melt temperature than normal wax, and generally it is melted over direct heat, unlike other waxes. It "melts" at between 180 to 220 degrees Fahrenheit.

This type of wax is always used for container candles, as it does not harden. The containers need to be heat resistant, just as containers used for other candles. The finished candles sustain a higher temperature than normal candles, and burn at about 260 to 280 degrees Fahrenheit. If you choose to color your gel wax, use a liquid dye, as it mixes better with the oily texture of the gel wax. It takes only a little bit of dye to dye gel wax. If you want to add scent to your gel wax, make sure it is oil soluble and considered candle safe.

Wax Additives

There are additives that you can buy if you are having troubles with your candles. These additives can help with mold release, luster, pliability, and color conservation.

- Luster crystals will provide your candle with sheen and make it burn longer. You don't need to use a lot of these crystals to do the job. Most luster crystals recommend 1 tsp. per pound of wax.

- Snow wax adds an opaque, high luster quality to your wax and prevents the candles from melting or sagging in warm weather. It improves the texture and burning time of the candle as well. As with luster crystals, use only 1 tsp. per pound of wax, but melt it separately from your candle wax and then add it into your melted wax.

- Microcrystallines are used to refine the properties of your wax. There are two types of microcrystallines, though there is a wide variety of these two types. The first type increases the flexibility of your wax so that it can be used for modeling. It also makes it easier for the pliable wax to stick to other pliable waxes while making models. The second type works the other way making the wax harder to increase the sturdiness of your candle. However, if you add more than 2% of this additive to your wax, you may encounter problems with your wick and the way it burns.

- Snowflake oil is a decorative element that produces a snowflake effect in the finished candle. This is used on many aromatherapy candles that you can purchase at stores.

- Stearic acid is added to wax, generally paraffin to increase burning time and give it a more opaque look. It's recommended to use 2 to 5 tbsps. per pound of wax.

- Vybar makes your candle harder, more opaque, and decreases the shrinkage that sometimes takes place as the wax cools. It also works as a fixative for added scents. It is recommended that you use 2 tsp. per pound of wax, but no more than that. You can start slowly, adding 1 tsp. to your first batch to see if it helps.

Wax Temperatures

The temperature you melt your wax at has a lot to do with the container (or lack of container) that is being used to create your candle. The following temperatures work best with the candle type and mold type. In some cases, as in the make-your-own cardboard mold, the low temperature will prevent the mold from falling apart or burning.

Type	Temperature (degrees Fahrenheit)
Acrylic Molds	180 – 210
Bayberry Candles	130
Containers Candles	160 – 165
Dipped Candles	155 – 160
Glass Molds	170 – 200
Metal Molds	180 – 210
Rubber Molds	160 – 180
Taper Candles	158
Tear-away Molds (such as cardboard)	160

Chapter 5: Using Your Own Beeswax

If you keep bees, or know someone who does, it's a simple process to take beeswax and process it. If you aren't using it already, or if your friend will sell you raw beeswax, the following section will guide you, step-by-step, through the process of creating useable beeswax from the gooey cluster you get straight from the bees.

When harvesting honey, beekeepers scrape the honey straight off of the honeycomb. This process teaches you how to harvest the beeswax off of the honeycomb. If you are already harvesting honey, then you have the honeycomb in hand. After the honey has been removed from the comb, set them aside until you have a good supply. If you are buying the comb from a friend, the honey will probably already have been removed.

1. Soften and clean your honeycomb by soaking it in warm water to wash off any leftover pollen and honey. You may need to repeat this part a few times.

2. Break the comb into manageable chunks and place the chunks into water that is just above the level of all of the chunks.

3. Heat the honeycomb over low heat, stirring constantly. When the wax is melted, remove from heat. Don't spill any—like all wax products, honeycomb is highly flammable.

4. Pour your beeswax and water into a fine mesh bag. You can use nylon or sacking—as long as it is heavy duty and has small pores. Don't overfill the bag, as you need to tie it at the top.

5. Holding the bag over a bowl, squeeze from top to bottom to push the wax through the pores. This will leave any bee pieces or flotsam in the bag, refining the wax.

6. Place your bowl in a dust-free place and let cool. As it cools, the water will separate from the wax. If any wax sticks to the bowl, throw it out; it will contain the debris that remained and settle to the sides or bottom of the bowl.

Note: You may need to repeat this process a few more times to get rid of all of the debris from the bees' occupancy. To repeat the process, remove the hardened wax from the bowl and repeat steps 2 through 6. On the last pass through this process, skip step 6 and go to step 7.

7. Take a soapy dishrag and smear another bowl with the soapy water. Set this bowl aside.

8. Squeeze the reprocessed beeswax into your soapy bowl. You can use non-scented to retain the smell of the beeswax, or you can use scented soap—it is completely up to you.

9. Let the wax cool for 12 hours without moving it around. Again, make sure it is in a dust-free area.

You now have beeswax. You can melt it again to make hand dipped candles, container candles, shoe polish, crayons, lip balm, or skin ointment.

Chapter 6: Types of Candles

Once you have mastered making simple candles, you may want to try other kinds that you may want to have a go at. The possibilities and types are endless. I have listed a few here for you to become acquainted with.

Pillar Candles

These are basically candles that have a very solid shape and can stand without any help. They are often found in churches and other places of worship and are most commonly found in a cylindrical shape. There are, however, many variations of this candle type. Pillar candles can be bought in square, rectangular, and even hexagonal shapes and they can be small or huge. The bigger sized candles will often have more than one wick.

Floating Candles

With the ability to float on water, these candles make a perfect decoration piece. They tend to be very small with smooth, simple, and elegant shapes. These shapes do not have to stick to a prototype; they can also be extremely extravagant shapes, such as seashells and sea horses

Votive Candles

Small in height, votive candles do not go above 2 ½ inches high. They are the type of candles that are bought in small glass containers, usually in a cylinder or square shape. The reason for them being sold inside a glass container is due to the liquidity of the wax, which would otherwise spill everywhere once melted.

Taper Candles

These are the candles you will normally see on dinner tables or in candelabras. Taper candles have a very long, sleek profile due to them being about ¾ inches in diameter and range from between six to eighteen inches in height.

Container or Filled Candles

Non-flammable wax with a wick in the middle is set in a container, which is completely resistant to heat. For example, glass jars are often used as containers for container candles. These types of candles can be very adorable.

Tea light Candles

Tiny and elegant, these candles' prime purpose is to be used in food or oil warmers. These candles are even smaller than votive candles.

Gel Candles

Transparent in color, these come in a huge variety of shapes. When you see these candles for the first time, you will not recognize them as candles. These tend to come in containers, but some can be made more rigid to be free standing by using additives.

Birthday Candles

This is one of the most common candles, and the one thing without which no birthday party would be complete. These come in various shapes and sizes that range from tiny sticks to chunky letters, and they're something we all love.

Chapter 7:   Selling Your Candles

You may be wondering, why sell your candles? Candles have a very low investment rate for the amount of product you can create. For instance, you can buy a ten-pound slab of paraffin wax for about 25 dollars. Since 1 pound of paraffin melts down to 20 oz. of liquid wax, if you made 12 oz. candles, you could make about 16 candles out of that 10 pound slab. Most 12 oz. specialty candles can sell anywhere from 15 to 25 dollars a candle. Once you have the recipe down and are able to make creative, sensational candles, you can easily make back your original investment, plus a hefty profit. Selling just two of your special candles will earn back most of the money you spent on supplies, including essential oils, wicks, and dyes. You can make your own molds or even use items from your trash as a container. For instance, if you have any nice bottles lying around, and you had a way to cut those bottles (you can most likely find a service that does this; check your local college's art departments), you could create a unique container candle.

Candles not only sell themselves, but can be very fun to make and require a minimal amount of labor. Therefore, if you have a passion for making candles, you have a ready-made product that can be launched into the market immediately. However, this does not mean that you will have the opportunity to sell your candles to each and every person successfully. It also does not mean that you will become a millionaire; however, it will provide you with some spare cash without putting in too much time or effort. Another thing to keep in mind is that this should start as a side business, unless you have extreme dedication or are able to lure friends into your business. This business is great for people with flexible hours who need a little bit of spare change.
Of course, nothing happens like magic. There is no business wizard just waiting for you to step out with a unique candle and make you rich. It takes a lot of hard work and dedication to make your side business into a profitable, full-time career.

In Person

One of the major questions where starting a candle business is when to start selling your product. The best way to determine this is by finding out where your market lies. Anywhere you can find your customers is the perfect place to sell your candles. There are, however, some tried and tested selling spots that always tend to yield success.

Choosing a Venue

There are a lot of different venues in which you can sell your product. You can sell your candles just about anywhere, from flea markets to fairs to farmer's markets. Finding the right spot is the first step, setting up your booth is the next.

You can try selling them at flea markets, though you will find you will not receive the highest price in this area. However, if you do not mind haggling, flea markets or swap meets are good places to begin to sell your candles. It can get frustrating when people offer too little money for something you've worked so hard on; however, if you are ready for this kind of market, they are a great place to generate cash, as well as to create a customer base. This venue can open you up to a whole new way of thinking. It can be a testing ground for new scents, colors, and candle styles. It can be a field in which to test a company name or product name. Once you have sold your products at a few flea markets and gotten your business name cemented and your product line solid, you can move on from there. You can also sell in tandem. A lot of flea markets are weekends only, so you can sell here during the weekend, and at other places throughout the week.

Some charities will allow you to sell your candles at their charity events. You can give them a discount on your candles for an auction or some other fundraising event. While you may not make a lot of money on this venture, what it will do is get your product and company name out there. It will expose people to your product, and if it's a good product, they may contact you for more. If you do donate your candles for a charity event, be sure that your company information is part of the package. You should have your business name and a way to be contacted (or a website link) printed on your labels.

Another venue to try is your neighborhood farmer's market. Most cities host a farmer's market in certain spots on certain days, so you may have to move from place to place on a daily basis. The best way to start selling at a farmer's market is to speak to the people who run the market. Different cities have different rules, but if you are using all natural products and local goods to create your candles, that can be one of your main selling points. While people may think "produce" when hearing the term farmer's market, there is a variety of non-food related merchandise available at most markets. If you happen to live in a city with a dedicated market, like Seattle's Pike Place Market, you can rent a stall by the month, though you will probably not be lucky enough to get one inside the market.

You can also rent booths at all sorts of fairs and conventions, as long as your product fits with the convention's theme. For instance, if there is a home decorating event at your local fair grounds, you may be able to rent a booth there for the weekend and sell your candles to individuals who are specifically in the market for decorative goods. Most State Fairs also allow people to rent booths to sell products. That's one of the ways they make their money. The money from the booth rental usually goes to the fairground, not the carnival that happens to be traveling through. It takes a lot of research and out-of-pocket expenses to sell your products at fairs and conventions, but it will be worth it in the long run.

Creating Your Booth

After you have decided upon your selling platform, you need to make your selling area eye-catching in order to pull in those customers. Your setup and display is vital when it comes to selling your candles .If it is an outdoor fair or event then it is very likely that you'll have a canopy to shelter your products and yourself from adverse weather conditions or to provide shade during very sunny days. Seeing as you will be selling your candles, the sun will be more of a concern than the rain, as you do not want your product to melt. Ensure that you always have a canopy with you that is not too bulky or difficult to setup, such as those backyard canopies in the event that one is not provided for you by the event committee. The best kind of canopy is a 10 by 10 instant canopy. These can be a little on the expensive side, but when it comes to ease, they are well worth the investment. These canopies will hold up for years to come and are perfectly sized for about ninety nine percent of the stalls at most events. The vertical nature of their legs also insures that no valuable selling room is taken up on your booth, as the table will be inside the canopy and not supporting the canopy. If you are intending to stay in the candle business long-term, a 10 by 10 instant canopy is not only highly recommended, but it is also a mandatory part of your sale's kit.

Keep sandbags with you, as well, so that the wind does not blow your canopy around and ruin your display. Four sandbags, each weighing 20 pounds minimum should be sufficient for your needs. If you do not weigh your canopy down, you could end up chasing it all around the venue, as well as causing some serious damage to it and the hapless victims in its path of destruction. If damage is caused to your canopy, it will only result in you having to shell out some more cash to get new one. The sandbags are also essential when your booth is located on the pavement, as there will be no place to dig pegs into for the canopy.

It is highly recommended that you carry two tables to the venue. This will ensure you have a backup in case one breaks and also allow you to have a display on one table and work with cash on the other. The best types of tables are the type that fold up and are roughly 32 inches by 70 inches. Lay the tables out in an L-shaped it manner is the best configuration, as it allows for customers to be able to access products on both tables easily. An L-shape will also allow your booth to fit into smaller areas. In the end, it will be the allotted booth space that decides what shape you will be able lay out your tables in, but it is always a good idea to have a rough design planned before entering the venue. When choosing tablecloths, there are many aspects that you will need to consider. It is never good to have a messy, stained or dirty tablecloth, as it will give off a bad impression on the quality of your merchandise. Try to choose darker colors in the off chance that you do end up with stains or mud on your cloth .A darker color will mask these blemishes a lot more efficiently than a light-colored tablecloth. Never use a tablecloth that is patterned; you do not want to distract attention away from your product. If you distract the attention away from your candles, you will make fewer sales. Don't use a tablecloth that is made from fabrics that require extra care. Finding something that can easily be thrown into the washing machine and ironed quickly is ideal. This will save you a lot of hassle in the long run. Due to the odd size of your tables, your cloth may need to be custom-made. Make sure that you or the person sewing your cloth has a neat hand, as shabby work will only drive away clients .It must also lie flat, as any ripples or creases can cause your display to be continuously knocked over since they won't be able to stand straight. A slight wave or frill at the edge of the cloth also adds a nice little touch.

Even though fabric tablecloths are great and really pretty, it is simply easier, more efficient and cleaner to use plastic tablecloths. Remember, when using plastic for a tablecloth, make sure it is heavy duty to avoid unsightly rips, tears and scuffs. Just like fabric tablecloths, plastic tablecloths must lie flat on the table without wrinkling, rippling or creasing. To ensure this does not occur, always roll up your plastic tablecloth after use. Vinyl fiberglass is the best type of plastic to be used when choosing plastic tablecloths. This is because it is not only available in a variety of colors but it also lies flat and is completely wrinkle proof. This vinyl is readily available at most window dressing shops.

Signs are an important way of attracting customers. You will have competition with a lot of vendors, the number of which can go up to the hundreds depending on the locale. There are many schools of thought when it comes to designing the sign for your candle booth. One thought is that if you do not have a sign, people will stop at your stall out of mere curiosity and this could potentially be a sale. This is true when it comes to various products, but it is a better idea to announce to the customers what you are selling and how much you are charging. Remember to always put your sign in front of the canopy and in a place where all the customers can read it. Try having two or three signs, so that they can be read from various angles, and therefore, pull in more customers. Do not use fancy lettering or difficult to read logos, as this will only confuse the customer making them likely to walk away. When creating your sign, use simple, bold lettering in bright, contrasting colors. Make sure your lettering is large enough to be seen from the other side of the aisle.

Remember, you do not only need signs telling customers what you are selling, but also various information signs. You'll need a sign that is clearly showing the prices of various products, as well as any relevant tax information. Make sure you display the mandatory information that is required of you by to the local law of your area. Clearly mark your different products and give information on the places that you will be selling at if you move to different venues. Business cards also a great way to ensure that customers get all of your details that they require in order for them to keep in contact with you. Put these somewhere near the front of your stall to make them easily accessible to customers, as well as passersby.

If you are allowing customers to design and make their own candles, and your area is covered over by a canopy, ensure you take all the safety precautions required to protect you and the public from serious injuries. A rope or sign is not sufficient, you will need to make some sort of physical barrier to keep people, especially younger children, at a safe distance. A lot of people ignore signs and ropes and let the children do as they please on family outings, so on the unfortunate occasion that something happens, it is you who will be blamed, and it is your business that will come into disrepute. Accidents cannot be stopped; you can only make precautions in an attempt to prevent them from occurring. Ensure that your table is sturdy and will not tip over, especially if you have a double boiler running. Using Plexiglas as a barrier is also a very good idea. It is preferable that this Plexiglas is placed toward the front of the stall for optimum safety measures. Try weighing everything down with sandbags to make sure nothing moves about.

On Consignment

There are also several stores that have a handmade candle section; try talking to them about selling your candles within their store. This will work best in areas with high tourist levels. However, you may also find gas stations or smoke shops that allow you to sell your items on consignment. There may also be local stores that allow people to sell items on consignment. Call the store and ask for the store manager to get details on their consignment programs and disburse your product through many stores. At this point, you should have a company name and a label for your products that contain your contact or website information. Remember that if you are selling them on consignment, the store gets a cut of the profits.

Online

Other than real-life opportunities, you can also sell your products on the Internet. It will not give you as much interaction with your customers as other venues do, but it will allow you to reach out to a wider audience. If it is the Internet route you choose to take, once you have created a customer base, you can create your own site, which will help eliminate overhead costs, such as the fees you have to pay to the various websites.

You can sell them on websites that are dedicated to auctions or crafters, such as Ebay.com or Etsy.com. You may also make your own website, but you will need to advertise. If you choose to sell them on EBay or Etsy, you can set your own prices. EBay has a choice called, "Buy it now" in which you can sell your items for a certain price, and people can just click "buy it now" instead of bidding on them; however, they only remain on sale for a limited time, and the candle will need to be re-listed if you do not sell out. Etsy.com allows you to set your own prices, and the items will remain on sale until sold. Both sites require that a part of the sale goes to them. That's how they make their money. If you make your own website, you don't have to worry about paying another person, and all the funds can go straight to you. You can always advertise your sites (Etsy, EBay, or your own webpage) on places like candle making message boards, forums, and Craig's List. This will not only make your hobby more satisfying, but it will also allow you to make extra money.

Chapter 8: Candle Making Books and Videos

Here are a few books and videos that you may find helpful when you begin the adventure of candle making. This is not an extensive list, and it is not even close to what is available on the market. Books and videos about candle making and cover nearly every relevant candle topic you can think of. If you can't find it in a book, check online.

Books

- Candles by **Betty Oppenheimer**, March 1, 2004.

- Profit by **Michelle Espino**, July 27, 2000.

- Guide by **Sandie Lea**, July 15, 1999

- *The Everything Candlemaking Book: Create Homemade Candles in House-Warming Colors, Interesting Shapes, and Appealing Scents (Everything Series)* by **M. J. Abadie,** May 1, 2002.

- Dummies by Ewing, November 5, 2004.

- Time by **Jennifer Furgeson,** February 3, 2010.

- Beeswax by **Rebecca Ittner,** August 2, 2011.

- Time by Vanessa-Ann, March 28, 2004.

- Started by **Eric Ebeling**, 2002.

- *Candle Making: 16 Stylish Projects from Start to Finish (Step-By-Step Crafts)* by Owen, December 1, 2001.

- Home by K M S Publishing.com, Dec 31, 2009.

Videos

There are many videos available about candle making from candle making websites and you tube. The following list, however, are videos you can purchase, rent, or check out at your local library.

- Making, Starring Marie Kauffman and Noreen Hill, November 19, 2007.

- Guide Starring Sharyn Pak, June 14, 2010.

- *Making Candles with Mabel* DIY

- Making Starring *the West Ladies*, November 15, 2008.

- Candles, Starring Marie Kauffman and Noreen Hill, December 13, 2007.

- *How to Make Candles: Secrets to Candle Making Success* with Jenn Spencer

Websites

- CandleWic—http://www.candlewic.com. *This website sells candle making supplies and a section dedicated to helping beginning candle makers learn the craft.*

- Michaels—http://www.michaels.com/Candle-Making%3A-Everything-To-Get-You-Started/as0096,default,pg.html. *This is Michael's, a nation-wide craft store, own webpage. This page is a list of everything you need to get started on your project. It includes wax types, what type of wicking to use for each type, what type of scents, dyes, and containers to use. It takes out the guesswork for you.*

- Candletech—http://www.candletech.com. *This site gives easy to follow directions for fun and unique candles. It shows you how to make your own wax melter by converting a Presto Kitchen Kettle into a melter that has a spigot, reducing your supply list. It also has various recipes for using leftover wax, creating Halloween candle decorations, adding embellishments, making cupcake candles, and fun holiday ideas.*

- About.com—http://candleandsoap.about.com. *You can find instructions for everything on About.com and candle making is one of them. This page teaches you about supplies, safety, decorating, and gives you project ideas. If you have a question that needs answered, you will probably find it here.*

Chapter 9: More Tips

Here are some tips to ensure that your candles come out the way you want, and you are safe in the process.

- Do not light candles until they have cured for at least 24 hours.

- Never melt wax directly over heat. Wax likes to start on fire when it gets too hot, which can be very dangerous to any candle maker. Always use a double boiler.

- Do not try to put out a wax fire with water; instead smother it with a blanket, baking soda, a lid, or a towel.

- Clean up spills as they happen. Melted wax is easier to clean up, and melted wax near a hot burner is a fire hazard.

- Don't pour unused wax down the drain, as it will quickly cool along the sides of the drain and clog it up.

- Don't try to wipe off hot wax that has spilled on your skin, as the wax adheres to skin and wiping it off can cause tearing. Instead, run cold water over the wax to cool it and then just scrape it off.

- If you spill uncolored wax on your clothing, let it harden and then scrape it off. You can also use a paper napkin or facial tissue and an iron to remove it. Place the paper napkin on both sides of the stain and iron. However, if the wax is dyed, take the garment to a dry cleaner as they are better prepared for this incident.

- Waxy residue can be removed from your equipment by freezing the items. The wax will become loose and will be easily removed.

- Save all of your candle leftovers as they can be used again and again. Let friends know that you are saving leftover candle pieces and ask that they collect them for you as well.

- It is essential that you stir continuously when the candle wax is melting when you are adding dyes and oils. In order to make sure that constant stirring occurs at the correct time, always keep a stirring utensil at hand.

- Mold releases are essential, especially if you're a beginner. It will prevent having to scrape the candle out from the mold and ruining it.

- Make sure that you read the packaging of your wax to see if it is a single pour or double pour. It is a very simple, yet regularly made mistake by beginners, to use double pour wax in the same manner as single pour.

- Wax will always splatter when poured into the mold. To protect your work surface, always line with waxed paper or some kind of protective covering.

- For a perfect candle and to ensure there are no hiccups, weigh your wax. This will save a lot of waste.

- Make sure you use enough wax to get the intended color, too much or too little could result in a color you do not want.

- Remember to steer clear of adding perfumes to your candle for scent purposes. Perfumes are flammable so can cause a whole load of trouble.

- Just remember you will not get the perfect results the first time. Just like everything else, candle making is trial and error so keep a record and keep on trying. You will get there eventually.

Burn Rate

The amount of wax that the wick melts in grams on average in an hour is known as the burn rate. The more the wax consumed, the higher the burn rate. Always remember that it is not only the type of wick used that affects the burn rate, but it is also the fragrances, colors and containers that affect the burn rate. It is always recommend that you perform a test burn.

It is very easy to perform a test burn. Simply begin by weighing your candle before lighting it. Burn the candle while timing how long it is been left to burn. After doing this, blow out the candle and reweigh it. You are now ready to perform the calculation. Start by taking the original weight of your candle and subtract the weight after burning. Divide your answer by the number of hours your candle burned. You now have the burn rate per hour. Divide the original weight of your candle by burn rate per hour to give you the burn rate in hours.

For example, you weigh your candle at 16 ounces before burning, you burn it for 3 hours and reweigh it, and it is now 15.5 ounces. First, you subtract the beginning weight and the ending weight: 16 oz. – 15.5 oz. = 0.5oz. in 3 hours. Split this number by the number of hours you burned it: 1 hour, in this instance, would equal 0.16 oz. burned. Next you divide by original weight by the per hour burn rate (0.16). This will give you a total burn time of 100 hours.

If you wish to calculate the burn rate for container candle, do not forget to weigh your container before pouring in the wax to set. When you weigh the set candle, remember to subtract the container weight from the total weight. You can then follow the instructions above.

Some Tips When Working with Gel Wax

Gel wax is new to the market, and due to this fact, many candle makers find it very difficult and testing to work with, especially when it comes to essential oils. A lot of the essential oils will cause the wax to become clouded and may not bind to the wax properly. This is due to a low flashpoint of the fragrance. Always remember to select a fragrance with the minimum flashpoint of at least 170 degrees Fahrenheit when using them with gel waxes. Many essential oils may also be tinted, and this will affect the color of the candle, even if you are attempting to create a clear candle. It is a good idea to experiment with a small amount of wax, fragrance, and color before creating a whole candle.

Gel waxes also have the annoying tendency to form bubbles while cooling. To avoid this, make sure you melt the wax on high heat with as little stirring as possible. Another way of avoiding bubbles is to increase the temperature of your wax to 225 degrees Fahrenheit if you are using dyes and fragrances. After using these tips, if you still find that there are bubbles in the candle after it has been poured into the mold, try putting the molds into the oven at 200 degrees Fahrenheit until the bubbles have completely vanished. You could also put the candle out in direct sunlight; this will also help remove bubbles.

Always use unprimed wicks for gel candles as a primed wick can cause clear candles to appear cloudy. For gel candles, prime the wick with the gel wax before use.

Embedding Items in Gel Wax

Gel candles work the best when simple. Try putting them in glass containers of various colors to give them even more appeal. You can also decorate your gel candles using various items as long as they're not flammable. To embed an item, begin by pouring a small amount of wax, then dipping your items in the wax to prevent bubbles before placing them into the melted wax. Try to keep the items as close to the edges of the container as possible. This will ensure that the items are seen, as well as kept away from the wick. Continue layering your wax and adding objects until you get the desired look. Make sure that you do not overcrowd the candle with too many objects, as you will not give the wick enough wax to burn.

Using Essential Oils and Colors with Gel Wax

Ensure that you use just the right amount of fragrance, as too much can cause your candle to spark when lit. If in the unfortunate case your candle does begin to spark, melt it and add more wax. To ensure optimum safety always read the label of fragrance oils and dyes to ensure that they are correct for using with gel candles. Do not ever use any substance that is not designed to be used in a gel candle.

How to Choose a Glass Container

When choosing a glass container, make sure it has a minimum of a 2 inch diameter. This will allow the heat generated to be evenly distributed, and it also ensures that the wick and flame are as far away from the glass as possible. Ideal places to find these containers are charity shops, garage sales, and various thrift stores. You can find treasures at bargain prices at these places. Things such as wine glasses, Mason and jam jars, vases or candy bowls make great candle containers; just make sure that the glass is not too thin, otherwise it will shatter due to heat.

Tips for Cleaning Up

Cleaning up is always the worst part of any job. Extra wax will be one of your biggest difficulties. The best way of dealing with it is by allowing it to cool and storing it in a resealable bag. This can then be thrown out if you do not want to keep it. To remove any oily residues, try using some form of Windex on the all surfaces. Scrub the Windex off with hot soapy water. You can also freeze the individual items to loosen the wax.

Safety

Always remember to never leave melting wax unattended, especially if there are small children in the house. Melted wax is very hot and can cause serious burning. Another thing to be certain of is the thickness of your glass container. Glass that is too thin can be easily shattered when excess heat is applied. Also, do not pour hot wax into a very cold glass container. The sudden influx of heat can also cause the glass to shatter.

Keep your hot wax far away from plastic or flammable containers, as they can melt or ignite.

It is best not to let the candle burn until the very end, as this can cause extremely hot glass to break. And it goes without saying that the candle should never be left burning unattended, otherwise all hell can break loose.

Chapter 10: Troubleshooting

No matter how hard you try or how exacting you are, problems will arise. This section will guide you through some of the more common problems that occur when you make candles and help you fix the problems in subsequent batches.

Problem: Wick Burns Straight, Leaving a Cavity in the Center

This is when the flame burns the wick straight down the middle of the candle, leaving the sides up. It can make it hard to keep the flame extinguished. This usually happens when you are using a hard wax in large diameter pillar candles. Use a softer wax or only use hard wax for smaller diameter candles.

Problem: Candle Changes Color

There are two things that can cause the color of your candle to change, sunlight or hot wax. If you add your color to your wax when the wax is too hot, the color will fade. If you are going to color your wax, avoid heating it above 190 degrees Fahrenheit. If your candle is exposed to direct sunlight, the color will fade. A lot of colors tend to fade in the sunlight. You can purchase UV protective wax additives to stop the sunlight from leaching away the color so quickly.

Problem: Candle Won't Burn

You light the wick, and it won't take flame. The cause of this is that you used a wick that was not primed. Prime the wick that's sticking out with melted wax or hold the candle upside down over an open flame and allow the melted wax to prime your wick.

Problem: Candle's Surface is Cracked

This is usually caused by cooling the wax too quickly or leaving it in the freezer for too long. It's best to let the candle cool slowly to avoid cracking the wax. If it's a pillar candle, you may not have used a wick that was big enough, which can cause it to crack.

Problem: Candle Drips

Candles should burn slowly, allowing the melted wax around the wick to slowly evaporate as they are heated. This helps any scent permeate the air best. If your candle is dripping excess wax, and there isn't a draft around, the problem is either with your wick or your wax.

- A wick that is too small might not be able to absorb the wax that is melting around it.

- The wick could be the wrong type or size for the blend of wax you used.

- The wick may not be centered properly, causing it to burn on one side more than the other. Check the position when the candle is out, and if possible, re-center it manually.

- The wax may have been too soft or had a melting point that was too low.

Problem: Candle Stops Burning

You are enjoying the tranquility of your candle and suddenly, with no draft or further prompting, the flame sputters and goes out. This can be caused by using wax additives of inferior quality that can possibly clog the wick. That's why it is essential that you check all ingredients and their quality before purchasing them.

Problem: Candle Won't Release from Mold

Your candle is done cooling and it's ready to come out of its mold. You turn it upside down, and it doesn't budge. You put it in the freezer for a while, turn it upside down, and it doesn't budge. What went wrong? This is where you retrace your steps.

- Did you coat the inside of the mold with a mold release? If not, this step is essential and shouldn't be skipped. Mold release helps the candle slide out.

- Did you use a lot of beeswax? Beeswax is extremely sticky and doesn't shrink while cooling. A high percentage of beeswax can make the candle difficult to remove. Beeswax works best for non-container candles.

- Did you pour the wax into the mold when the wax was at a high or very low temperature? Make sure you keep the temperature of your wax at its required heat level for an optimal pour.

- Did you overfill the second pour? If you did, the wax that was meant to go into the indent may have expanded to the outside of the candle. Make sure you re-pour slowly to avoid overfilling.

As a last resort, try running hot water over the mold. This may help it release, but it could also cause defections in the candle's look. If it does, try over dipping the candle to fix any problems.

Problem: Excess Wax is Left on the Container Walls

Container candles should be left lit for at least four hours. When you keep them lit for smaller periods of time, it doesn't allow the wax to burn completely, leaving it on the walls of the container. It may also be left on the walls of the container if you don't use a container wax or a wax with a low burning point. Another cause could be that your wick is not the correct wick for the container.

Problem: Outside of the Candle Looks Dusty

The candle may have been sitting in storage for a while and doesn't have its like-new luster. Polish the candle with an old pair of nylons or use almond oil to renew its shine. You could also over dip the candle to renew the shine.

Problem: There are Pits and Bubbles in the Wax

Pits and bubbles can mar the look of any candle, and there are many causes for these conditions.

- Wax was poured too quickly. Make sure you pour your wax at a steady pace, and after you've finished pouring, tap the sides of your mold to help release any air that may have gotten trapped during the pouring process.

- The mold was dirty. If the mold is dirty, even slightly dusty, it will cause pits to appear in the candle's exterior. Make sure you are using clean molds.

- Wax was too cold or too hot when poured. Either increase or decrease the temperature of the wax. Make sure you keep notes, which will help you figure out the possible causes.

- Too much mold release was applied to the mold. Use your mold release according to the manufacturer's directions and avoid using excess mold release.

- A small amount of water may have gotten into the wax while it was being poured. Sometimes, the boiling water of a double boiler may bubble over into your wax bowl/pan. Make sure that your wax bowl or pan covers the opening of your boiling pan or is high enough that it isn't easy for water to get into the wax.

- The candle may have cooled too quickly. Make sure that you have your candles cooling on a wire rack to allow it to cool from the bottom first. Candles should not be crowded together on this rack, either, but kept at least 2 to 3 inches apart.

- Too much of your essential oil blend was added, diluting the wax mixture too much.

- The wax or melting pot was dirty. Make sure you clean all pots before use. Clean dirty wax by melting and then pouring through cheesecloth.

Problem: Colored Layers Bleed

You've created a candle that has layers of colors, but when it cools, you can see the different colors through the layers. You may have re-poured when the wax was too hot or done it too soon. Don't add a new layer until the first layer has formed a rubbery surface, and reduce the pouring temperature if it was too hot.

Problem: Mold is Leaking

This is more than likely due to the fact that you didn't seal the wick-hole at the bottom of the mold well. You can use mold sealer generously, unlike mold release. You can use as much as you need to seal the hole. Also, be sure that your wick is straight and taut.

Problem: There are Dark Spots on Top of the Candle

You may not have mixed your dyes completely in the wax, the wax could be dirty, or you used a pigment instead of a dye. Pigments should only be used for over dipping and not for solid colors.

Problem: The Candle is Mottled

If you are using essential oils, you may have used too much. You can purchase additives for the wax that helps disburse the oils throughout the candle. This can also be caused by the wax cooling too quickly or the use of too much mold release.

Problem: The Flame Sputters

Nothing ruins the mood like a candle that keeps threatening to go out. This can be caused by excess water in the wax, oil or air pockets in the wax, an unprimed wick, or too much of a spicy essential oil. To prevent these problems, make sure that no water gets into your melting wax or that your container isn't wet (even on the outside) before pouring the wax into the mold. Make sure that the container you are using to pour your wax is also dry. To prevent air pockets, tap the mold or poke a skewer around the wick immediately after pouring to release excess air. Make sure you are priming your wick before using it. If you are using a spicy essential oil, use the minimum amount possible for the amount of wax.

Problem: Sides of Candle Cave in

This problem is usually caused by air bubbles. Tap the mold and skewer near the wick immediately after pouring to release air.

Problem: The Candle is Smoking

Smoke isn't good for anyone or anything. If the problem isn't caused by a draft, which makes the candle burn hotter, it may be due to the wicking. Make sure you are using the appropriate wick for the candles size. It should not be too thick, too long, or the wrong type for the wax to blend.

Problem: The Flame is Weak or the Wick is Drowning in Wax

This can be caused by a wick that is too small or too loose. Also, make sure your wick is the right size for the melting point of the wax used. It could also be because you used too much stearic acid or other additives. Use less next time to see if it prevents the problem.

Problem: Wax is too Brittle

If you find that your candle's wax is chipping, you may have used too much additive, too many different types of additives, or your storage area may be too cold. An easy fix for your next batch of candles would be to use fewer additives, and only a few at a time. Store candles in an area that is between 44 and 70 degrees Fahrenheit.

Problem: There are Visible Lines on the Outside of the Candle

This is usually caused by the use of too much stearic acid, a mold that is too cool, or a pouring temperature that is too low. Use less stearic acid—follow manufacturer's directions. If you did, use less than they recommend next time. If your mold is too cool, preheat it before pouring in the wax. Also, make sure that the wax is poured at the correct temperature.

Problem: The Scent of the Candle is not Strong Enough

Not everyone's nose smells the same, so what works for you may not be enough for others and vice versa. This can be caused by many different factors that are easy enough to fix.

- You didn't use enough of the essential oil mixture. Try using at least 1.5 oz. of essential oils per each pound of wax at first.

- You used too much vybar (see **WAX ADDITIVES** for vybar's description). The recommended amount of vybar for one pound of wax is only 1 teaspoon.

- You used a cheap, low quality fragrance instead of an essential oil or you used a cheap, low quality essential oil. That's why it's important to ensure that the oil you are purchasing is well-made and natural.

- You added the essential oil too soon. Make sure you wait until the last possible instant before adding your essential oil to the melted wax, just before pouring.

- You used a scent that was not made for use in candles. Make sure you are using essential oils that are compatible with wax.

- Your candle's scent isn't apparent from the outside layer. Rubbing the outside of the candle should help release the scent to that layer.

- Before deciding if the scent is strong enough, allow the candle to burn for at least one hour before proclaiming judgment. This will allow the burn pool to form, which is where the scent is primarily risen from.

- If your burn pool is not large enough (at least .25 to .5 inches deep in 4 to 5 hours), make sure you are using the correct wick size and type for your wax blend.

Glossary

Bayberry Wax
> Bayberry wax is created by boiling the berries from the bush. The wax is sage-green in color and has a natural, spicy aroma.

Beeswax
> Natural wax created from the wax found in the honeycomb. Works well in hand dipped candles and container candles.

Braided Wicks
> These wicks are also referred to as core-less wicks. The fibers are braided together and are not braided around a core.

Burn Rate
> The amount of wax that the wick melts in grams on average in an hour is known as the burn rate. The more the wax consumed, the higher the burn rate.

Candle Dye
> These are dyes that are added to the wax to create your desired color. These come in block, powder, and liquid forms.

Candle Molds
> Molds come in various shapes, sizes, and properties. These must be able to withstand the heat of melted wax. Do not use molds that have not been prepped.

Candle Thermometer
> This is a thermometer that goes up to at least 220 degree Fahrenheit. You can substitute a meat or candy thermometer.

Candle Wick Tabs
> This is the small metal tab at the bottom of a candle. These can be purchased separately from the wick and attached to the wick of your choice. Some wicks come with the tabs pre-attached.

Candle Wicks
> These are used to light the candle and must be primed before use.

Chunk Candles
> Candles made up of different sizes or shapes of chunks of wax.

Container Candle

A container candle is any candle that is poured into a container. It is not meant to be taken out of its container. Do not choose a container that is flammable.

Cored Wicks

Cored wicks are wicks that tend to be braided with a core of cotton, paper or zinc to help keep the wicks upright.

Cotton-Core Wicks

Cotton-Core Wicks are also best in the above candle types. They create a slightly curled flame that creates an even burning circumference. It doesn't smoke as badly as the paper-core variety.

Double Boiler

A bowl or pan placed on top of another pot of boiling water. This is a process used mostly for melting easily-scorched liquids like wax or chocolate. It allows the product to melt without introducing direct heat.

Essential Oils

Scents added to wax to create an aroma when the candle is burned. Essential oils should be natural for best aroma production.

Floating Candles

These are candles that are placed in bowls or cups of water for an attractive effect.

Gel Candles

Candles made from gel wax. The wax usually has a thick, liquid texture.

Gel Wax

Gel wax is made from mineral oil, but it has been thickened with a polymer, creating a smooth wax that has a longer burn rate than paraffin or natural waxes. It is generally clear in color, but color can be added to it.

Hand Dipping

This is the process of candle making in which wicks are dipped into the melted wax to create the candles.

Liquid Dye

This is the concentrated liquid color for wax.

Luster Crystals

It adds sheen and a longer burn rate to the candle.

Microcrystallines
> Type one increases flexibility of the wax for use as modeling wax. Type two increases hardness of the wax.

Mold Release
> This is any agent that will allow the candle to slip out of the mold when cooled. They are available for purchase from most craft stores.

Mold Sealer
> This seals the mold to prevent leakage. It is generally used on the bottom of the mold where the wick is inserted.

Overdipping
> Taking an already-made candle and dipping it into colored wax to add new layers to the candle. You can also use this technique on candles that have been damaged as a way to salvage the damaged candles.

Paper-Core Wicks
> Paper-core wicks are usually used for votives, tea lights, and container candles. They smoke more than other wicks, however.

Paraffin Wax
> Paraffin wax is made from mineral oil. Works well in molded candles and has a higher melting point than most natural candles.

Pillar Candles
> Free standing candles, generally in the shape of a pillar. These can be thick and squat or thin and long.

Powdered Dye
> A coloring used for wax that is in a powder form; it is usually dissolved in stearic acid.

Repour Wax
> The wax you add to your candle after it has cooled to fill in the sinkhole around the wick.

Scent Notes
> Each scent carries its own note. They range from the base note, the top note, and the mid note.

Snow Wax
> It adds an opaque, high quality luster and hardness to your candles.

Snowflake Oil
> This is a decorative element that produces a snowflake effect in the finished candle.

Solid Dye
> These are blocks or chunks of colored wax or pigments used for coloring wax.

Stearic Acid
> This is a solid fat derived from animals or vegetables. It is an additive that can increase opacity, hardness, and the clarity of your colors.

Taper Candles
> These are the candles you will normally see on dinner tables or in candelabras. Taper candles have a very long, sleek profile due to their being about ¾ inches in diameter and range from between six to eighteen inches in height.

Tea Light Candles
> Tiny and elegant, these candles' prime purpose is to be used in food or oil warmers. These candles are even smaller than votive candles.

Vegetable-Based Waxes
> Vegetable-based waxes are made from different bases. They can be made from soybeans, jojoba beans, palm wax, and other vegetables. Normally used in container candles.

Votive Candles
> Small in height, votive candles do not go above 2 ½ inches high. They are the type of candles that are bought in small glass containers, usually in a cylinder or square shape.

Vybar
> Makes your candle harder, more opaque, and decreases the shrinkage that sometimes takes place as the wax cools. It also works as a fixative for added scents.

Wax Additives
> These are added to the wax to create specific effects. See also: Luster, Snow Wax, Microcrystallines, Snowflake Oil, Stearic Acid, and Vybar

Whipped Wax
> The process of whipping wax to create a foamy, whipped cream-like texture.

Wire-Core Wicks

Wire-core wicks can also be used for container, votive, and tea light candles. Some can be purchased with tabs already attached. Most are made from zinc, but be aware that some may be made with lead, which can be a health hazard.

Printed in Great Britain
by Amazon.co.uk, Ltd.,
Marston Gate.